Wandering Educators Press

The Philippines: 100 Travel Tips

By Rissa Gatdula-Lumontad &
Dr. Jessie Voigts

Table of Contents

Preface

The Philippines – just think the word, and you're immediately transported to a modern paradise. The beaches, food, culture, and hospitality and friendliness of Filipinos are globally well-known. With this book, you hold an insider's guide to experiencing the best of the Philippines. It's a glimpse into a deep and complex culture that has a long, rich history. It's a jam-packed travel guide to the best of the Philippines. And, it's written by a Filipino with a deep love of country. We're proud to publish this with Wandering Educators Press – and share the Philippines with our readers.

Dr. Jessie Voigts, Publisher,

WanderingEducators.com

Introduction

Born here. Raised here. And, unless there is anything that comes up that will compel me to leave, will probably die here. I love the Philippines!

I've known as early as grade school years that we have 7,107 islands and so many provinces that each had its own "culture." But few know how exceptional and diverse our attractions are. Traveling to different locales will show you the genuineness of Filipino hospitality, which makes me proud to be a Filipino.

Yes, I so LOVE the Philippines! I love our people. I love our nature. I love our culture. I love our food. I love our weather. I love our brown color. I love our "English." I could go on and on. But you will probably only be able to understand if you yourself have experienced our country.

So allow me to help you through your journey to discovering why "It is more fun in the Philippines." And maybe... just maybe... you will also learn to love our islands.

The Filipina contender for the Miss Universe title in 1994, Charlene Gonzalez, was asked "How many islands are in the Philippines?" Without batting an eyelash, she responded with a question, "Low tide or high tide?"

Located in the western Pacific Ocean, the Philippines is a Southeast Asian archipelago of 7,107 islands (during high tide, per Charlene). The country has an area of approximately 300,000 square kilometers (120,000 square miles) and has the 5th longest coastline in the world at 36,289 kilometers (22.549 miles). Because of its geography, it is endowed with diverse natural attractions, both land and sea, which makes it a fascinating destination for tourists.

The Philippines is composed of three major island groups, geographically distinguished as Northern (Luzon), Central (Visayas), and Southern (Mindanao), each with its own distinct attractions. The capital, Manila, is located south of Luzon.

Aside from its physical beauty, the Philippines also prides itself of being the largest English-speaking nation in the region, making conversing convenient for visitors. The major enticements, however, are the genuine hospitality and inherent fun-loving nature of the Filipino people. The latter was the anchor of the new Department of Tourism slogan, "It's more fun in the Philippines."

Here are **100 Tips for Travel in the Philippines** – allowing you to make the most of your stay.

WHEN TO VISIT

The Philippines is generally a year round destination. There are periods that are best for a visit, depending on your priorities. Here are some of things that you should consider in planning when to go.

1. ***Go during the winter months.*** North Americans and Europeans who have visited the Philippines consider it to be a tropical haven. If you want to take a break away from the freezing cold winter season, then the Philippines is one of your best options. Being a tropical country, the hot and humid climate is a welcome retreat from the chill back home.

2. ***Visit between December and February to enjoy the coolest weather, or between March and May to frolic under the summer sun.*** The Philippines has three seasons: a hot dry summer season from March to May; rainy from June to November; and a cool dry season from December to February. Coming during the cool dry season is best, especially for first-timers. However, if you are used to having hot dry weather in your place of residence, then there is less chance of getting shocked by the heat during summer.

3. ***Avoid the holidays and peak periods.*** Resorts usually have peak rates, normally during the Christmas and New Year holidays,

Chinese New Year holidays, and Holy Week holidays. Visiting before or after these holidays will both allow you more breathing space and to benefit from savings on accommodation.

Filipinos have acquired a culture of travel, so expect an incursion of domestic tourists, especially during school breaks, which are during the Christmas season and between April and May. The Holy Week, All Saints Day, and All Souls Day (November 1 and 2 respectively) are also vacation time for the locals. Those in the cities travel to visit their relatives in their hometowns or schedule trips out of town. Domestic flights, ferry trips, and provincial bus trips are always full during these times. Thus, it is highly recommended that you schedule your trip around these days.

4. ***Avail yourself of tour package promotions and special offers during the low season.*** Some popular island destinations like Boracay have low season rates, usually between September and mid-November. If you want to catch these resort promotional packages, then this is a good time to go. However, remember that this period falls during the rainy season. Also important to note is that the Philippines sits across the typhoon belt, and about nineteen typhoons enter its area of responsibility a year, about eight or nine of which make landfall. Be ready then for possibility of getting stranded for a night or two if staying in the island resorts.

5. ***If shopping is your pleasure, come during the period after the commercial holidays.*** Shops come out with crazy after season sales promotions after Christmas and Valentine's Day. The Filipinos also celebrate Easter, Halloween, Mothers' Day, Fathers' Day, and many other holidays, so sales offers are all over town. There are also payday sale promotions which are on the 15th and end of the month.

6. ***Time your visit during festivals for more fun.*** The Philippines, being a predominantly Catholic country, observes religious holidays with much fervor. It is famous for having the longest Christmas celebration in the world. Christmas carols are in the air and Christmas decorations are up as early as September. Furthermore, each city or municipality has its own "fiesta" in honor of a patron saint. There are also thanksgiving festivals the whole year round. If you wish to experience the fun of these colorful celebrations, then check the Department of Tourism website (http://www.tourism.gov.ph/) for the calendar of events to decide which most interests you, so you can schedule to come during the period.

WHAT YOU NEED TO ENTER

7. ***Make sure your passport is valid for six months upon arrival.*** This holds true for most countries, including the Philippines.

8. ***Plan to tour the country within a visa free stay.*** Most foreign nationals are allowed 21 days to visit the Philippines for business and tourism purposes. Check out the Department of Foreign Affairs website (http://dfa.gov.ph/main/index.php/consular-services/visa) for a list of countries. If you plan to stay longer than 21 days, make sure to process an extension of your entry visa 7 days prior to the expiry.

HOW TO GET THERE

The Philippines is well linked to many cities in the world, so it is easy to get to. Find out the best ways to get there and choose with what you'll be most comfortable.

9. ***Fly to the capital, Manila- the most strategic entry point.*** Several international air carriers, including United Airlines, Delta Air, Swissair, Lufthansa, Cathay Pacific, Malaysian Airlines, Singapore Airlines, Air France, Emirates, and many others fly between the Philippines and major cities of Asia, Australia and New Zealand, North

America, Middle East, and Europe. The national capital of Manila is the major international gateway, with its Ninoy Aquino International Airport (NAIA). The airport has three terminals: NAIA 1, which is the oldest and accommodates most international carriers; NAIA 2, which is exclusive to the national flag carrier, Philippine Airlines; and NAIA 3, the newest, which handles the other Philippine carriers, Cebu Pacific Air, and Airphil Express. Domestic flights, taxis, buses, ferries, and private car rentals are available from the city to destinations not only within Luzon but all over the country.

10. ***Avoid the hustle and bustle in Manila by entering via Cebu.*** If you are planning to explore the Central and Southern islands, then you can opt to enter via the Mactan Cebu International Airport (CEB) on Mactan Island in Cebu, the second major entry point. Flights from Australia, Hong Kong, Japan, and Singapore come to Cebu. Cebu is

considered the hub of Central Philippines and has a good connection to other destinations in the region, as well as to other parts of the country via air travel, ferry, or bus.

11. ***Connect from other Asian countries to Central Luzon.*** If you are planning to visit another Asian country together with the Philippines, then you may take the budget airlines that fly into the Diosdado Macapagal Airport in Clark from Hong Kong, Thailand, Malaysia, Korea, Singapore, and Macau. Aside from lower fares, Clark is a good entry point if you are planning to explore Central Luzon. Chartered flights from Hong Kong and Taiwan also fly to nearby Subic International Airport. Both Subic and Clark are a convenient two hours drive to Manila. Subic was the site of the U.S. Naval Base, the largest installation in

the Pacific, while Clark was the site of the U.S. Air Force Airbase, the largest overseas military installation of the United States Armed Forces, until the early 1990's.

12. ***Fly to Laoag from Taiwan or Macau.*** If you wish to explore the heritage sites and the highlands of Northern Luzon, then you can enter via the Laoag International Airport in Ilocos Norte. Regular flights from Taiwan and Macau are serviced by this airport.

13. ***If the exotic Southern Philippines is your cup of tea, then you may want to consider flying to Davao International Airport.*** The airport currently services flights from Indonesia and Singapore. Davao City is the premier city of the south and is well connected to Northern and Central Philippines via air, ferry, and bus.

WHAT YOU CAN AND SHOULD BRING

Visitors to the Philippines may bring in duty free personal belongings, a maximum two cartons of cigarettes or two tins of pipe tobacco, and one liter of alcoholic drink.

It is advisable to:

14. ***Bring cash and major credit cards.*** Although most foreign currencies can be

exchanged upon arrival, it is safest to bring US dollars. However, limit your cash to maximum US$10,000 or its equivalent in other foreign currency, as there is a restriction in carrying in and out of foreign currency. Exchange some of your foreign money at the banks or authorized money changers at the airport upon arrival to cover porterage, transportation to your hotel, and tips.

You will need to change more at your hotel, banks, or at authorized money changers that abound in the tourist areas, as most establishments accept only the local currency. Be careful though when dealing with money changers, and make sure to count your money before leaving the counter. Major credit cards are widely accepted in shops nationwide, except in remote areas. Travelers' checks are accepted only at big hotels and department stores.

15. ***Bring a plug adapter and voltage converter or transformer for your electronic equipment.*** The electric plugs in the Philippines are usually two-prong, either flat blade or with two round pins. Some hotels have three-prong outlets, or provide adapters for guests. To be sure, it is best to bring your own adapter. Further, the electricity in the Philippines is 220 volts at 60 cycles per second, thus if your equipment specification is 110 volts, you will need a voltage converter - particularly if staying in the remote areas and in small hotels. Only some big hotels provide 110 volts outlets. Be careful when plugging in your equipment. It is better to be safe than sorry!

16. ***Bring a tri-band, open line, SIM-capable cell phone.*** Nearly all Filipinos have a cell phone, even those in the rural and most depressed areas, and mobile communication is the rule. A cell phone is indisputably the most convenient and practical means to stay connected while in the Philippines. You can purchase a local SIM upon arrival at the airport. Most come with free text messaging and voice call minutes, so you can use it immediately. You can even get a SIM with free data services such that you can maximize your phone's internet capabilities while in the

country. The service is cheap, and you don't get charged for incoming call or text messages. It is also very easy to reload your SIM, as load is available even at the small stores.

17. ***Bring enough of your prescribed medicines.*** If you are taking maintenance medications for any ailment, it is advisable to bring enough for the trip, or at least check prior to departure if they are available in the Philippines. Remember to bring your prescription from your doctor or hospital.

18. ***Bring your preferred toiletries if you are sensitive.*** If you are picky with your toiletries, then it is best to bring your supply from home unless you are sure they are available in the Philippines. Bring lots of sunscreen and insect repellant as well, although you can get these in the major department stores. For

women expecting their monthly period during their trip, bring tampons, as they are not easily available in the Philippines.

CULTURAL REMINDERS

The Philippines, having gone through Spanish, Japanese, and American colonization, plus a huge Chinese migrant population, has a fairly rich cultural mix which is progressive and relatively easy to adapt to. There are certain things, though, that the visitor must keep in mind when in the country.

19. ***Don't decline an invitation outright.*** Did we mention the Filipinos may be the most hospitable people in the world? Do note that they might feel offended if you refuse an invitation to share a meal or drink. Take a

rain check if you are not up to it at the time the invite is received.

However, learn to distinguish a polite invite from a real invite. For instance, it is customary for someone you find eating his lunch to invite you to join him. His not doing so is considered rude, in which case you can graciously decline with a "thank you."

When invited to someone's house for a private dinner or get-together, remember to bring a small gift, suitably food or drink, as a sign of appreciation. If invited to a party to celebrate a birthday or other milestone, a gift for the celebrant is appropriate.

20. ***Don't get involved with politics and religion.*** Refrain from discussing politics and religion in public. This may be a good thing to remember when traveling not only to the Philippines but anywhere else. You can never be too sure of who is listening, and it is best to avoid confrontations.

21. ***Never flaunt your nationality or superiority, even when you are upset.***
People worldwide, not only Filipinos, are sensitive about racial discrimination, and you should avoid any allusion to a race being superior in any instance. Arrogance is loathsome anytime, anywhere. Remember, you are a visitor and must learn to respect the locals, as you are in their territory.

22. ***Greet with a handshake or a smile.*** A handshake or a smile is generally accepted as a form of greeting. In some social circles,

greeting with "beso beso" - your cheeks touching the other's cheeks is the norm. Just follow how the others, in the group you are in, do it.

23. ***Show respect for elders.*** The Filipinos have high regard for their elders and you are expected to exhibit the same. Filipinos use "opo" (yes) and add "po" when responding to anyone senior. You may not be expected to use these phrases, but greeting the elders first during a meeting and addressing them with "sir" or "ma'am" are expected, unless you are told not to.

24. ***Do not call people by their first names unless advised that you may do so.*** It is proper to address people using their last names, such as "Mr. Cruz" or "Miss Garcia", unless they tell you that they prefer for you to call them by their first names.

25. ***Never point your finger at someone.*** Pointing your finger at someone you are talking with, or using your finger to call someone's attention, is considered insulting and may provoke a nasty situation. Always keep your fingers in check!

26. ***Don't get too upset or offended if someone is late.*** There is such a thing as "Filipino time" which came about because Filipinos were notorious in being late. It has come to the point that the time indicated on an invitation card will sometimes be an hour earlier than the actual event. Industrial development has brought about significant improvement in this aspect in the past decade and the situation is not as before, but still, it is best to be forewarned...

27. ***Don't be offended if you are called "Joe" or thought of as "American" even if you are not.*** Despite the influx of Caucasian tourists and immigrants from different parts of the world, many Filipinos, particularly those in the rural areas, would still consider any "white" man as American. The children

would greet you with "Hi Joe!" which is rooted from the American occupation. Just smile - and if the timing is right, then you may correct the impression.

28. ***Do give tips.*** Except in establishments where tipping is expressly prohibited, tipping, although not mandatory, is generally expected at hotels, restaurants, service establishments, and by taxi drivers. Check your bill if a service charge is included, which may mean you need not give a tip, though a small token or gratuity would still be nice.

LANGUAGE

The national language is Filipino (basically Tagalog), the language in Manila, its metropolitan area, and the Southern Luzon provinces. Be wary that there are 120 to 175 languages in the Philippines, owing to its geography, and that the next town may speak a different language from the first. Most Filipinos know Tagalog, although those in the remote areas may not be fluent.

Travelers will, without a doubt, find it easiest to communicate with locals in the Philippines among the other Southeast Asian nations. Still, you may want to consider the following tips:

29. **Speak in English.** Conveniently, English is a second language and Filipinos, even in the remote areas, can understand and speak at least Basic English. If your main language is other than English, and you are not conversant in the universal language, now may be the best time to learn the basic phrases.

30. **Learn a little of the vernacular.** As in other places, it will be good to know some phrases of the local language. It might be helpful to understand and speak some of the

basic Tagalog phrases like "Kumusta?" (How are you?) and "Salamat" (Thank you). If you plan to try the local public jeepneys in Metro Manila, then you need to learn to say "Para" (Halt or Stop). You will get smiles of approval in return.

31. ***Learn some Visayan phrases if going to Central and Southern Philippines.*** The Visayan language is predominantly spoken in Central Visayas and some cities and provinces of Mindanao. "Kumusta" is also used to ask how someone is doing. It might be helpful to learn "Maayo" which means "Good". "Salamat" is combined with "kaayo" to express thanks. Conjugation, both in Tagalog and Visayan, can be a little tricky.

WHAT TO WEAR

The Filipinos are generally casual dressers, perhaps because of the humid climate. They do dress up for important business meetings and functions and formal occasions, though. Men have at least one "Barong Tagalog", the national costume which is an embroidered shirt made of thin, cool native woven material. The fibers used are: piña, from pineapple leaf, and usually used for more formal occasions; jusi, from abaca or banana silk; and banana. There are less formal variations of the shirt like the "Polo Barong" which is short-sleeved, and "Gusot Mayaman", literally translated as "rich crumple", usually made of linen fabric. The less formal "barongs" are usually used for everyday business attire.

Filipino women rarely don the national costume, the "Baro't Saya" and its variation, the "Maria Clara", these days except during very formal occasions. The modern Filipina prefers contemporary gowns, as they may be more comfortable than the national costume. Some fashion designers would still pattern their creations on the traditional clothing and use indigenous materials, coming out with innovative attire with refreshing twists.

Planning your wardrobe should not be difficult. Read these tips below for guidance:

32. ***Bring light clothing.*** Clothing fit for a tropical climate is recommended. The Filipinos dress casually and a pair of modest shorts and a t-shirt is acceptable attire almost anywhere. However, take note that there are fine dining establishments and night spots that implement dress codes, and may require long pants and closed shoes. If going inside churches or to a business meeting, conservative, modest attire is deemed proper.

33. ***Have a set of formal attire on hand.*** Filipinos are well-known for being extremely hospitable. It is not unusual to receive an invitation to a party even after a first meeting. So it is best to be ready. Or, instead of bringing a coat and tie or a formal dress, you may just purchase a "barong" when the need arises. There are "barongs" for women, too, which are fashioned into dresses or blouses to be worn with dark skirts or pants. You may find the "barong" more comfortable than the layered formal attire you are used to back home, plus you will certainly delight your host when he sees you wearing the national costume. Just don't forget to wear a cotton

undershirt as it is see-through, else you will create a stir instead of pleasing your host.

GETTING AROUND

All forms of air, land, and sea are available for domestic travel. Check out your options below:

34. ***For utmost convenience and privacy, take a taxi.*** Taxis are everywhere in the urban areas. They are metered and lately are required to issue receipts. Make sure the driver flags down the meter as soon as you enter. It is illegal to refuse a passenger or to negotiate a fixed fare in the Philippines, but don't be surprised if you encounter a driver that will do so. It is best to take taxis from the major establishments like hotels and malls as they have people who assist you in getting one. There are taxi queues in some malls. Be sure you are in the right queue, as there are some with designated routes, either going North or South of the city. It is fine to give a few pesos in addition to the meter registration as tip to the driver if you are happy with his service.

35. ***Keep some change handy for bus,
    jeepney, and tricycle rides within the city.***
    Have a mini-adventure and try the most
    popular public transport in the Philippines,
    the jeepney, which has become a familiar
    symbol of Philippine culture. It is a colorful
    adaptation of the U.S. military jeep from
    World War II. Don't be surprised to see the
    driver accepting and giving change while
    maneuvering through traffic! People usually

shout "Para!" (Stop!) when they need to get off. Some tap the jeepney ceiling to let the driver know they are at their destination and want to get off.

City buses ply the route of Epifanio de los Santos Avenue (EDSA) and other major thoroughfares. Allow for longer traveling time than if taking a private car, taxi, or the MRT or LRT though, as they tend to linger at the bus stops to take on more passengers.

On side streets, you may see tricycles - motorcycles attached to a passenger cab. You can choose to pay for a private trip or squeeze in with other passengers and pay the fare for one person. These vehicles are not allowed on the main roads, although you may see one or two occasionally defying the rule.

In the remote areas, expect to see motorcycles, called "habal-habal" with a bunch of people on board. You will marvel at the driver's balancing skills! Passengers can also be seen on tricycle and jeepney rooftops in far-flung locales, particularly in mountain barangays.

36. *Take a bus for provincial trips.* Buses are the more common means of public transport for longer routes. If you have the time, and want to save a few pesos, take a bus to the provinces. Believe it or not, you can get from Luzon to Mindanao on a bus!

Danedherson.Garcia2012

In between islands, the bus gets on "Roro" (roll on, roll off) ferries. Note that sometimes the bus fare does not include the "Roro" fare and you may need to get a ticket for the ferry. When the ferry reaches the next port, passengers re-board and the land trip continues, until there is need to cross water between islands again.

Aside from being more economical, taking a bus also gives you more opportunities to see the countryside than flying.

Although vendors selling drinks, candies, and snacks are usually allowed to board the bus to cater to passengers, and the buses stop at restaurants for breakfast, lunch or dinner, it is best to bring your own bottled water and a snack on board. For overnight trips, there are buses that have reclining seats and a toilet on board. Check with the transport provider first before buying your ticket. Usually, tickets are purchased at the terminals, but you can call ahead to inquire about details so you are prepared for the trip.

37. **_Take the MRT or LRT in Manila to avoid heavy traffic._** If you are in a hurry to get

from one point to the other within Metro Manila, the MRT (Metro Rail Transit) or the LRT (Light Rail Transit), depending on your destination, is the best way to go. It is definitely faster as well as cheaper than taking a taxi. Be prepared to line up for a few minutes to buy your ticket, notably during the rush hours (between 7:00 to 9:00 a.m. and 5:00 to 8:00 p.m. during weekdays). If you think you will be using this means of transport often while in the city, it is advisable to buy a stored-value card to avoid the long lines.

38.   ***Take the train from Manila to Southern Metro Manila cities.*** The Philippine National Railways operates a commuter rail service for the Manila metropolitan area called the Commuter Express, also known as Metro Commuter or Comex. It is a cheap and traffic-free way to get to Southern Metro Manila from its Tutuban Station in Tondo, Manila City. It has 50 trips per day (25 trips per way) that traverses the cities of Manila, Makati, Taguig, Parañaque, Las Piñas, and Muntinlupa. The first northbound morning trip starts from the town of Biñan in the province of Laguna, while the last southbound trip in the evening ends in the town. The ride should be an exciting adventure for the visitor, as it passes through local communities and gives you a different perspective of life in the suburbs which you won't see otherwise.

39. ***Take an overnight sleeper train from Manila to Bicol in Southeast Luzon.***
Recently, the Philippine National Railways relaunched the "Bicol Express", a 10-hour trip from Manila to Naga. The train offers convenient sleeper accommodations and can be a cheaper alternative to taking the plane to Naga. From there you can go to Camarines Sur, one of the top tourist destinations in the country. This should free you of one night's hotel accommodation as well, or a total of two nights if you take the train round-trip.

40. ***Rent a car.*** Like in most urbanized countries, you can rent a car in the Philippines upon arrival. You can pre-arrange before you arrive with Avis, Nissan, or other rent-a-car companies, or book through your travel agent. You can get a self-drive car as you are allowed to drive using your foreign driver's license for up to 90 days upon arrival.

Remember that the Philippines is a left hand drive country. But be pre-warned! Driving in Philippine roads, particularly in Manila, can be a startling experience for a foreigner and you may be better off in hiring a vehicle with a driver.

41. ***Fly to other destinations from the major hubs.*** There are several flights between Manila, Cebu, Davao, and other airports to the other islands. You can book your flights early online. If you plan to stay long and want to visit many islands, you can register for domestic airline promo announcements so you can avail yourself of the lowest fares. You can also use travel agency services for your domestic ticketing requirements if you do not have online access and do not have time to purchase your ticket at the airline offices. Note that travel agencies may charge a

booking fee for issuing domestic tickets, which should be fine in exchange for the convenience and service.

42. ***Visit a combination of islands by taking small sea craft.*** Bangkas or pump boats, small wooden boats usually with bamboo outriggers, are the common means of transport between islands. You can go island hopping on a bangka. They vary in size, from one that can accommodate 3 persons including the boatman, to one that can accommodate as many as 30 to 50 persons. Some even have toilet facilities. Take note, though, that a bangka ride exposes you to the elements so it is best to splash on sunscreen before a ride, and bring protective accessories.

Some destinations have fastcraft services available, like between Cebu and Bohol. These are safe and reliable ferries that are faster than the regular ferry, shortening travel time almost by half. They are air-conditioned and even offer movies and magazines on board. There is usually a service counter where you can order food and drinks during the trip; that is, if you are the type who can take sea trips *sans* nausea.

43. ***Try the inter-island ferries.*** Again, if you
    have time to spare, you may want to try
    taking a ferry from Northern Philippines to
    Central or Southern Philippines. This is good
    if you are in the country during the dry
    season. These ferries provide air-conditioned
    cabin accommodations, meals, and
    entertainment on board. Do not expect
    facilities and service to be on par with cruise
    ships, though. Nevertheless, since you have
    nowhere to go but around the ship, you will
    have the opportunity to learn more about the
    culture through interaction with the locals on
    board. You will also love the scenery on the
    way when the vessel traverses between
    islands (7,107 islands, remember?) and get
    some true blue rest when mid-sea. Know that
    this is for the experience and not for you to
    save money, as you may even spend more

than airfare if you are taking a private cabin during airfare promo season.

ACCOMMODATION

44. ***Pre-book your hotel.*** The Philippines offers a wide range of accommodations to suit every traveler's preferences. Take your pick from 5-star hotels in the major cities and deluxe resorts in island destinations to basic pension houses and budget inns. Prepaid bookings are usually lower than walk-in rates and it is always best to be sure you have a place to stay at least for your first two nights.

45. ***Settle for a lower category hotel in destinations where you expect to do a lot of day activities.*** For places where you will

be doing tours and will be out of the hotel exploring most of the day, then it is more practical to just book at a lower category hotel. Just make sure the hotel has the amenities you cannot do without, like air-conditioning or hot water in the shower.

46. ***If you are staying for at least three weeks, save on accommodation cost by booking with a condotel or self-serviced apartment building.*** Paying for a unit for one month rather than paying on a nightly basis may turn out to be a cheaper option. Furthermore, you can save on food by preparing your own and stocking on groceries in your unit, rather than dining at hotel outlets or restaurants every night.

47. ***Experience authentic island living by staying in cottages made of local materials in island destinations.*** Some

island destinations offer nipa hut or cottage type accommodations, with or without air-conditioning. There are some with very basic amenities, usually furnished with bamboo furniture made by the neighborhood carpenter. Some are elegantly furnished with world class contemporary furniture designed by world-recognized local artists like Kenneth Cobonpue of Cebu.

48. ***Feeling adventurous? Rent a tent instead of a room.*** Some mountain and beach resorts have allocated camping areas for guests who want to save on accommodation or simply prefer to stay in tents. Just don't forget to bring your anti-bug lotion if you do not want to be mosquito fare, particularly in the evenings!

49. ***Give "glamping" a try.*** The Philippines has caught on the "glamping" vogue. A few resorts now offer the option for guests to camp in style and provide big tents that you can walk through, beddings, some furniture, and even floor rugs! If you like the outdoors but want more comfort than the regular camping gear usually provide, then "glamping" is the way to go.

DINING

Philippine cuisine is an interesting blend of flavors from years of colonization. The Chinese, Spanish, Japanese, and American influences are evident in the food - an eclectic mix which promises a delightful treat to your palate once you allow yourself to indulge!

50. ***Have your pick of any cuisine in the urban areas.*** The major cities within Metro Manila, Baguio in the North, Cebu in Central Visayas, Davao in Southern Mindanao, and other popular tourist destinations have a wide array of restaurants that serve international cuisine. Craving for dim sum? Chinese restaurants abound. Want pasta and pizza for dinner? An Italian restaurant is around the corner, or you can order delivery by the many popular pizza franchisees. Steak and burger houses are everywhere. Spanish, Thai, Indian, Persian, Vietnamese, Mexican, Continental... name it, and there should be a place that serves the food you are looking for. There are even places that specialize in Vegetarian or Halal cuisine. However, do not expect the same if you are in the rural and remote areas, as there are not many options besides the native food.

51. ***Be prepared to eat lots of rice in order to enjoy a Philippine gastronomic***

experience. The Filipinos are a rice-eating people. They serve rice even during breakfast. Why, they even eat "pancit" (stir-fried noodles with vegetables, meat and shrimp) with rice!

There are many sandwich places and bakeshops at every corner, but the Filipinos consider bread as a snack. Nevertheless, there is no need to worry, as you will need all those carbohydrates when you go around - especially during the humid summer season, because you will surely sweat more than usual!

Maybe one reason for the rice consumption is that most Filipino dishes are best eaten with rice. So if you want to taste the local cuisine (you should), then you must be prepared to eat more rice while in the Philippines. The more popular local dishes, all eaten with rice, include:

Adobo: pork or chicken, or a combination of the two meats, stewed in soy sauce, vinegar, garlic, and pepper, considered the Philippine's national dish. Each region may have its own variation, so you can have adobo in every destination you visit and yet feel like you are trying a new dish every time. There are adobo sandwiches, too, for those who do not like rice.

Kare-kare: oxtail with banana heart (the flower of the banana plant), string beans, and eggplant in thick peanut sauce, served with *bagoong* (shrimp paste).

Sinigang: a sour soup made from tamarind or other fruit broth, with either fish or meat and vegetables, which is served as a main course. Filipinos would eat this with the broth spread on their rice, although maybe not during formal dining parties.

52. ***Have the stomach for more rice!*** Can you imagine having rice as a main course and then finishing off with a rice dessert? Every province has its own rice cake specialty and there is an endless variety of rice cakes that will be offered to you, especially in the rural areas. They are usually cooked with coconut milk so make sure your stomach can take it before indulging.

53. ***Feast on lechon.*** A Filipino buffet spread will not be complete without *lechon* or whole roasted pig. Every region has its own recipe but common in all the variants are the delectable, crispy skin and juicy, tender meat. In Luzon, lechon is served with liver sauce, while in Cebu and other places in the Visayas and Mindanao, it is served with soy sauce and vinegar.

Left-over lechon is usually cooked as *lechon paksiw*, which is a delicious viand and offered as a main course in some restaurants.

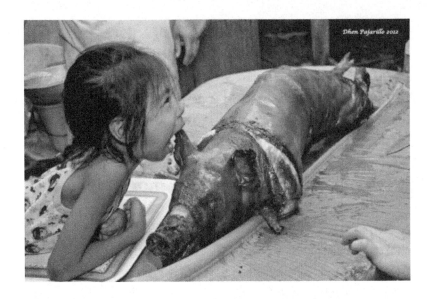

Most restaurant menus also have Lechon
Kawali and Crispy Pata in lieu of the
traditional roasted lechon. Chicharon (crispy
crackling), made from pork or chicken skin, is
also sold everywhere. These dishes give you a
taste of the crispy, juicy pork dish in case you
do not have the chance to try the "real stuff."

If you are hypertensive, have a heart
condition, or are watching your cholesterol
levels, you can take a small bite just so as not
to deny yourself of these mouthwatering pork
dishes.

54. ***If you are a heavy eater, take
advantage of the all-you-can-eat
establishments.*** All-you-can-eat restaurants
abound in the major cities. These are self-
serve dining establishments with a buffet set
up and charge a fixed rate. The only catch is
that you need to finish everything on your

plate, else you pay a higher rate. This is obviously their way of making sure diners only get what they can eat and avoid food wastage. There are restaurants that offer a few main courses for as low as Php199 per head. Some with a more extensive buffet spread charge higher.

55. **Have your fresh seafood cooked the way you like.** This is definitely an experience you should not miss while in the Philippines. The seafood is usually the catch of the day and is at its freshest. There are seaside places where you choose the seafood from a wet market then have the cook prepare your dish the way you want it. A whole fish can be made into 3 courses: soup using the head, grilled using part of the body, and kinilaw or the local version of sashimi, which is cubes of fish fillet dipped in native vinegar and some spices,

sometimes with coconut milk. A word of warning though... be ready to stare your fish straight in the eye, as fish is usually served with the head in the Philippines. If this grosses you out, tell the cook beforehand not to include the head when they serve the dish to your table.

56. ***Indulge and have your fill of fresh fruits.*** Taste the juiciest and sweetest fruits while in the Philippines. There are 88 varieties of bananas available year round! Mangoes, pineapples, papayas, and native oranges can be had any time of the year, too, but are sweetest during the summer season. Other seasonal fruits are watermelons, avocados, guavas, lanzones, rambutan, and many others. Exotic fruits like durian and mangosteen abound in Southern Mindanao. You should try calamansi, a small native lemon that makes a refreshing, sour juice drink.

57. ***Sample Jollibee fast food meals.*** This Filipino burger chain has proudly rivaled the international McDonald's chain and is present in many countries worldwide. Its recipes are made for the Filipino palate, such that spaghetti is sweet. Its fried chicken, Chicken Joy, is a favorite and preferred by many over the fried chicken at McDonald's. The servings are for a Filipino appetite, thus you may need to order double.

58. **Be ready to eat more than three meals a day.** The Filipinos are known to be food-loving people. They may not eat as much as others in one seating, but they eat the three major meals plus two to three snacks a day. An American motivational speaker addressing a Filipino corporate audience once remarked, "You Filipinos eat breakfast, snack, lunch, snack, dinner, snack, snack! It's a wonder you all do not weigh 300 pounds!" With all the eating and heavy meals, you definitely need to get out and explore while you are in the Philippines!

HEALTH AND SAFETY

59. **Get travel insurance that includes hospitalization and emergency repatriation.** Be sure that your plan includes emergency hospitalization while in the Philippines. There is no harm in having some form of surety.

60. **Get anti-malaria shots if traveling to remote destinations.** Don't leave home without anti-malaria shots if remote and highland places are included in your itinerary.

Eric Tanyen

61. ***Always have sunscreen and insect repellant lotions with you.*** The sun can be harsh, especially during the summer season, and mosquitoes abound in some outdoor places particularly in the evenings. It is critical that you stock up on sunscreen and insect repellant for your Philippine trip.

62. ***Never drink from the tap.*** Even the locals do not drink their tap water. There should not be a problem in big hotels and restaurants as they usually serve purified water. However, if dining at small eateries, make sure to ask first before taking any. If taking mixed juices, also check first if the water and ice used are purified. To be safe, just order bottled water, or always bring one with you. They are widely available except in very remote places.

63. ***Never leave your things unattended.*** As elsewhere, keep your belongings close to your person and beware of pickpockets, especially in shopping areas and crowded places. Never flash your cash or jewelry. Make use of hotel safety vaults for important documents like your passport and cash, and keep copies of your documents in case of loss or theft.

64. ***Be wary of strangers.*** This is a universal rule, taught to us since we were kids. It serves you best to be careful anywhere you go. Although the Filipinos are generally a friendly lot, there are still bad elements as in other places in the world, and it is sensible not to accept invitations from just anyone.

TRAVELING WITH KIDS

The Philippines is child-friendly and your kids will have a wonderful time here. As in traveling with kids to any other part of the world, take the usual safety precautions and you and your kids should be fine, and treasure your visit. Some tips that might be helpful:

65. ***Bring your kids' prescription and first-aid medicine and toiletry brands.*** Aside from the health and security concerns outlined above, be sure to bring enough supply of your child's prescribed medicines, as they may not be available in the Philippines. It will also be advisable to bring anti-diarrhea medicine in case of stomach upset. Always bring bottled water wherever you go. Bottled water is widely available for purchase.

In the same manner, it is best to bring enough supply of the toiletry brands your child is used to. They may not be available in the Philippines, or even if available, may not have the same exact formulation. Remember that the weather may be very different from where you are coming from and adverse reactions to the heat and humidity can happen. You would not want to aggravate this by using toiletries that your kid is not used to.

66. ***Bring a change of clothes wherever you go.*** Children coming from cold countries may have difficulty adjusting to the tropical weather. They may perspire more than usual, thus you should be ready with extra clothes when you are out exploring. A hand towel will be very useful in making sure that perspiration, particularly on a kid's back, is prevented from drying on its own.

67. ***Choose hotels with babysitting or child care services.*** You may want some time to yourself during your visit and it is therefore more convenient if your hotel provides child care services. In the provinces, you can even

hire a private nanny during your stay. Ask for referrals from your hotel, or better yet from friends or people you may know in the Philippines. Filipinos love children, so expect a lot of attention.

If traveling with more than two children or with those 12 years old and above, check first the availability of adjoining rooms and compare the rates with a family unit. Two adjoining rooms sometimes turn out cheaper than a family room. Check activities for kids hosted by your hotel.

SHOPPING

68. ***Check out the name brands in the malls and specialty shops.*** Most internationally famous name brands are available in the malls and specialty shops in every city or town. Some items may be cheaper than at your home country and you just might find a great buy specially during sale season.

A must visit is the SM Mall of Asia (MOA), located at the reclaimed area in Pasay City. It is a tourist destination in its own right. At 407,000 square meters, it is the Philippine's largest and the world's third largest mall.

Another world-class shopping area is the Greenbelt in the business district of Makati, with 5 malls that houses specialty shops, a wide variety of restaurants, coffee shops, and classy bars. It is connected to the Glorietta Shopping Center, the Landmark Department Store, and the SM Makati.

69. **Hunt for bargains and unique items at tyangge bazaars.** Bazaars called *tyangge* (market) are everywhere, particularly during the Christmas season. They are usually

composed of sellers in temporary booths who offer their wares at discounted or promotional prices for a certain period. You can find good bargains and stock up on unique holiday gifts during these fairs, as there are entrepreneurs who only sell their products at these venues.

70. **Take a shopping adventure in Divisoria.** Divisoria is known as a bargain hunter's paradise in Manila. You can find anything you need here, from clothing to furniture at unbelievably low prices. Be warned though that knock-offs are aplenty, sold on wholesale. But you are sure to find nice items, some imported from China, Thailand, and Indonesia. Make sure to haggle and get more for your money. Be prepared to squeeze in the crowd though, and be careful with your belongings. Avoid wearing jewelry when you are shopping here.

TOP ATTRACTIONS

It is best to pre-arrange your tours for a hassle-free vacation. To help you decide which among the 7,107 islands to include in your itinerary, below is a rundown of the top tourist destinations in the Philippines and their distinct attractions.

71. ***Metropolitan Manila and Environs.***
Starting with the basics may be the sensible thing to do on your journey to discovering the Philippines.

It is likely that you will come in via Manila and as such, should then explore the metropolis and nearby places. Ironically, the international airport is actually located in Pasay City, not in the city of Manila, as is generally believed. Pasay City is one of the 16 cities and 1 town that comprise Metropolitan Manila.

Metropolitan Manila, or simply Metro Manila, is the country's economic, political, cultural, educational, and social center. Thus, all the modern conveniences are within reach while staying in the Metro. A wide range of accommodation from budget inns to deluxe hotels abounds in Makati, Manila and the Ortigas Center area in Pasig City. Both Makati and Manila are just a few minutes' drive from the airports.

While in Manila, visit **Intramuros**, the "Walled City", which was the bastion of the Spanish colonial government in the 1500s. The walls tell the rich history of the city through the Fort Santiago, the defense fortress where the Philippine national hero, Dr. Jose Rizal, was incarcerated prior to his execution at Bagumbayan, adjacent to Intramuros, now **Rizal Park**. A monument of the hero watched by honor guards stands in memoriam.

Nearby is the **Quirino Grandstand** where many national celebrations are held, including the inauguration of incoming Philippine presidents.

At the Bay area, there is the **Manila Oceanpark**, a theme park featuring a giant aquarium and sea animal shows. There is also **Star City**, another theme park with thrilling rides and a Snow World where visitors can experience playing in the snow. Around the area are the **Cultural Center of the Philippines** where ballet, musical shows, and art exhibits are held, the **Philippine International Convention Center**, the **World Trade Center,** and the newest, the **SMX Convention Center**.

Don't miss watching one of the world's **spectacular sunsets** from **Manila Bay**. You can stroll along the bay with your trusty camera to document this stunning scene. If you time your visit on the second half of February, you should take time to see the PyroMusical Competition at the Mall of Asia grounds. It is an international event with spectacular fireworks displays by experts from different countries.

Chris Vergara|IMAGES

From the bay area, you can take cruises for Dinner and to **Corregidor Island**, a small rocky island fortress called **"The Rock"**, which stands as a memorial for the heroism of the Filipino and American defenders who stood ground against Japanese invaders during World War II.

In Makati, there is the **Manila American Cemetery and Memorial** where the largest number of World War II casualty is buried.

Close by are Dasmariñas Village and Forbes Park, where many of the rich and famous hold residence.

From Manila, you can take a relaxing drive to **Tagaytay City**, a favorite upland retreat for Metro residents. Here you get a majestic view of **Taal Volcano**, the world's smallest that is a volcano within a lake. You can visit organic farms, relax in one of the spas, take a cable ride, feast on fresh fruits, or just enjoy the cool breeze.

Other recommended daytrips from Manila are: **Pagsanjan Falls and Rapids** where you can "shoot" the rapids; **Hidden Valley** where you can rejuvenate in the natural spring pools and commune with nature in a verdant forest setting; **Villa Escudero** where you are introduced to a coconut plantation and lunch on a raft amidst a waterfalls backdrop.

Also south of Manila is the **Enchanted Kingdom**, a theme park with world-class rides and attractions. For those who wish to enjoy the sun, sand, and sea just a few hours ride from Manila, there are beach resorts in the southern provinces of **Cavite**, **Laguna** and **Batangas**.

72. *Banaue, Sagada and Northern Luzon.* Explore the awe-inspiring highlands.

Be amazed by t*he famed **Banaue Rice Terraces** in the Mountain Province in Northern Philippines, a UNESCO World Heritage site called the eighth wonder of the world. Marvel at this magnificent masterpiece our Filipino ancestors carved 2000 years ago. Trek down to an Ifugao village for a personal encounter with the locals.*

*A few hours' drive away is the idyllic town of **Sagada**, famous for its burial caves and hanging mummified coffins. Many artists have found wonderful inspiration in these highlands and some have made the place their home.*

You can try the seat-in coach tours (often called SIC tours, in which you join in a group with other tourists) offered by local tour operators which depart Manila on Thursdays and return on Sundays.

The 8-hour drive from Manila to Banaue may be long, but it passes through pleasant rural scenery in the provinces of Nueva Ecija and Nueva Vizcaya.

On the way back to Manila, you can take the route that goes to **Baguio**, the *Summer Capital* of the Philippines. Here, you can visit **Mines View Park** for a panoramic view of the Cordillera mountain ranges, **Camp John Hay**, a former U.S. base that is now a recreation facility, the **Philippine Military Academy** to see future officers of the Armed Forces of the Philippines in training, the **Tam-awan Village** for a glimpse at indigenous lifestyle, go strawberry picking at **La Trinidad** and shop for fresh vegetables, fruits, and souvenirs at the **Baguio City Market**.

If you have time, head to the **Hundred Islands National Park** in Alaminos, Pangasinan between Baguio and Manila, and go island hopping.

73. *Palawan.* Go nature tripping in this eco-tourism destination, dubbed *Philippines' Last Frontier.*

Christopher E. Cruz

Palawan prides of its mega diversity and recently earned international acclaim when the **Puerto Princesa Subterranean River National Park**, more commonly known as **Underground River**, was named one of the **New 7 Wonders of Nature**. The river is the longest navigational underground river in the world, and is one of the most important biodiversity conservation areas of the Philippines.

Puerto Princesa City in the central part of the province is the country's second largest city, yet is one of the greenest with lush tropical rainforests instead of the usual tall buildings you would expect in a city. You can stay at small hotels or at the many pension houses and inns that dot the city, and explore on board a tricycle (a motorcycle with a sidecar). You can also go island hopping in the pristine waters of **Honda Bay,** or see playful dolphins in their natural habitat at **Puerto Bay**. For a relaxing, get away from it all vacation, you can stay at the Dos Palmas Island Resort and Spa in Honda Bay.

Another point of interest is the **Iwahig Penal Colony**, known as the biggest minimum security prison in the world, where you can see orange-clad prisoners move around freely, working at the farms and handcrafting wooden souvenirs.

You can fly to Puerto Princesa from Manila or Cebu and easily be able to do all the activities above while staying in the city.

The **Tubbataha Reefs Natural Park**, a world heritage site and a premier dive site, is located in the Sulu Sea, about 98 nautical miles from Puerto Princesa City. Live-aboard dive safaris are offered by dive companies.

If you want to explore the rest of Palawan, it is best to fly from Manila.

Northern Palawan is known as a tropical paradise. Luxury island resorts like El Nido, Club Paradise, Club Noah Isabelle, and the very exclusive Amanpulo, a favorite hide-away of the rich and famous, draw tourists from all over the world in search of an ultimate getaway. The **Calauit Island Game Preserve and Wildlife Sanctuary**, located in northwestern coast, is also a primary attraction.

74. *Boracay.* Traipse on the white sand beach of Boracay, indisputably one of the best beaches in the world.

Boracay has been awarded by **TripAdvisor** as the **Travelers' Choice 2011** second best beach in the world, and is ranked fourth among the **Top 10 Islands** list in the **Travel + Leisure** travel magazine's **World's Best Awards 2011**. The island may be reached by flights from Manila to Caticlan or Kalibo. Boats to the island are stationed at the Caticlan wharf. You can pre-book your transfers together with your resort booking.

There is a wide variety of accommodations, from deluxe, butler-served resorts and spas to budget huts, and restaurants offering almost all types of cuisine. You are sure to find something to satisfy your fancy.

You can walk barefoot even during high noon on the white, powder-like sand, and the pristine waters are so clear during the summer months that you will think you are swimming in a man-made pool instead of a beach.

Aside from the usual water sports, Boracay boasts of a Graham Marsh-designed 18-hole par 72 golf course, and horseback riding, zorbing, zip lining, go karting, segway riding, and parasailing facilities.

For less than $20, you can get a massage on the beach, bring home several sets of pearl and shell accessories, walk on the seabed on a helmet dive, or have a seafood buffet meal!

In the evenings, Boracay turns into a party place for the fun-loving beach buffs, as the beach comes alive with live entertainment offered by the beachfront bars and restaurants.

If coming on the third Sunday of January, you can join the merry-making during **Ati-Atihan Festival** in **Kalibo** town on mainland Aklan. Dance to tribal music in the streets with contingents wearing indigenous costumes over charcoal painted bodies.

75. *Cebu and Bohol.* See the best of Central Philippines in one trip.

Cebu is known as the **Queen City of the South**, and is the main hub and center of commerce and education in Central Visayas.

It offers historical and natural attractions in a convenient urban setting.

The Portuguese explorer, Ferdinand Magellan, landed on Cebu's shores in 1521 and introduced Christianity to the natives. The **Magellan's Cross** stands as a monument to this historical event, alongside the **Basilica Minore del Santo Niño**, which houses the original image of the child Jesus that was gifted by the Spanish colonizers to the then Queen of the kingdom.

Also in Cebu City is **Fort San Pedro**, the smallest and oldest citadel in the country, built during the Spanish era and served as stronghold of the Spanish and later, the American settlers.

In downtown Cebu, the **Casa Gorordo**, the former residence of the first bishop of Cebu is now a museum, which showcases the lifestyle during the colonial period. In the neighborhood is the **Heritage of Cebu Monument**, a sculptural tableau that is an illustration of the symbolic events in Cebu's rich history.

For a breathtaking view of the city and surrounding islands, go up to **Tops**, located in Busay Hills, 2,000 feet above sea level. You may also want to visit the **Taoist Temple** in the upscale residential area of **Beverly Hills**, light a joss stick, and make a wish after taking in the scenic view from its highest level.

The international airport is located on **Mactan Island** in **Lapu-lapu City**, named after the Philippine's first hero, a monument for whom stands on the spot where the native king, Datu Lapu-Lapu, was said to have killed Magellan. Nearby is a row of seafood restaurants called **Sutukil** or **STK**, acronym for Sugba, Tuwa, Kilaw which is a local way of cooking fresh fish - grilled, soup, salad. You can buy fresh fish and seafood at the market, have a restaurant cook them STK or any way you like, and then dine while the gentle sea breeze caresses you.

Several beach resorts are on Mactan Island, from where island hopping and dive tours can be done. Bangkas can take you to the **Hilutungan Marine Sanctuary**, where local fishermen will guide you through the snorkeling area. If you are into **bird watching**, or simply want to see the life at a **fisherman's village**, visit **Olango Wildlife Sanctuary** on Olango Island, a sanctuary that hosts the largest migratory birds found in the country.

Excellent dive sites are found around **Mactan Island**, **Malapascua Island** on the northern tip of the province, and **Moalboal**, a town southwest of the province.

Oslob, a town in southeast Cebu province, offers an exhilarating experience as you interact with **butandings** (whale sharks) in their natural habitat. The whale sharks in the area are very friendly, most likely because they are hand-fed by the fishermen!

Souvenir hunters will find Cebu a treasure trove of handicrafts, especially those made of shell. You should also visit a guitar factory to witness the craftsmanship and musicality of the Cebuano.

You might want to consider coming around the period of the third Sunday of January, when the **Sinulog Festival** is held. It is one of the biggest mardi gras celebrations, with street dancing and religious parades held in honor of the **Señor Santo Niño** (child Jesus). Or, check out the Cebu Province website for the festival timed during your visit. Cebu, after all, is dubbed the *Island of Festivals* and all but four of its 9 cities and 44 municipalities have a festival celebration.

From Cebu, hop on a fast ferry to Bohol, a quaint island that offers an overwhelming myriad of surprises for its size. The countryside tour is a must do. It includes a visit to the **Chocolate Hills**, an extraordinary geological formation of at least 1260 hills that can be viewed from a deck on top of one of the hills. The site is the country's third National Geological Monument, and the hills are covered with grass that turns brown during the dry season, hence the name.

FERNANDO CALIZA

You will surely get wide-eyed like the **tarsiers**, as you are amazed while catching sight of them in their natural habitat. The adorable tarsier is the smallest primate in the world and is an endangered species.

Cruise the **Loboc River** on a floating raft and find peace with the tranquility of the riverside communities. A mellow serenade by local musicians on board is a pleasant bonus. And, if you are lucky, you can catch the **Loboc Children's Choir** in concert. The choir is multi-awarded internationally.

Watch local craftsmen as they labor to make **bolos** (Filipino knives similar to the machete) and **weave nipa** leaves for hut roofing and baskets.

For a sense of the province's heritage, visit **Baclayon Church** and **Dauis Church**, two of the oldest churches in the country.

Highly recommended is a visit to the **Bohol Bee Farm**. Make prior reservations for Dinner, which is guaranteed to be a tasty, filling spread of organic meats and vegetables capped with their famous squash muffins and home-made ice cream. Come early so you can have a tour of the farm and learn how bees are cultured. Make sure to check out the souvenir shop, as there are some nice and unique handicrafts - and bring home a bottle or two of their honey, fresh jams, and spreads. They can arrange shipment for you so you need not carry all the jars with you.

Bohol also lays claim to world-class dive sites. A marine sanctuary is located around the

Balicasag Island, a popular stop for divers and snorkelers.

76. *Ilocos Region.* Travel back in time on a heritage trail in Northern Philippines.

Stroll along the **Mestizo District** in **Vigan**, Ilocos Sur, one of the Hispanic towns left in the Philippines, and now a **UNESCO World Heritage Site**. Walk through the cobblestone streets of **Calle Crisologo** where colonial houses remain standing, most now serving as hotels and restaurants. Make sure to try the delectable authentic delicacy, the **Vigan empanada**, a pastry made from rice flour filled with Vigan longganisa (native sausage), vegetables, and eggs, from one of the vendors who cook them as you order from hawker stalls around **Plaza Burgos**.

Jim Bernardo

Take a **calesa** (horse-driven carriage) ride around the city and visit a **burnayan** (pottery) to see how Vigan jars are made.

Visit ancestral homes of legendary Ilocano personalities, like the **Syquia Mansion** (residence of the 6th Philippine President, Elpidio Quirino), the **Father Jose Burgos Residence**, and the **Quema House**.

From Vigan, take a two-hour drive to **Laoag**, Ilocos Norte, the stronghold of former Philippine President Ferdinand Marcos. On the way, visit the **Juan Luna Shrine** in **Badoc**, a reconstruction of the ancestral home of the patriot painter from whom it is named, and the remarkable church and coral formations of **Currimao**.

Make sure to check out the Spanish colonial architecture of the **Fort Ilocandia Resort Hotel**, the baroque and oriental architectural mix of the **Paoay Church and Belfry**, the **Marcos Museum and Mausoleum** where memorabilia of the late President's family are displayed and a tomb which houses his embalmed remains is open for viewing, the **Malacañang of the North** which was the official residence of President Marcos in Ilocos Norte, and the **St. William's Cathedral**, commonly called the **Laoag Cathedral**, with its astounding **sinking Bell Tower**.

For the adventurous, dare to go on a 4x4 sand board experience at the **Suba Sand Dunes**.

Jim Bernardo

Further north, take a break at the white sandy beaches of **Pagudpud**, known as the **Boracay of the North.** On the way, drop by the **Burgos Lighthouse** and the **Bangui Windmills**, a truly marvelous sight to behold.

77. *Davao.* Have your fill of superlatives in this Southern Philippines city.

Considered the Philippines' **Asian City of the Future**, Davao is the **largest city** in the BIMP-EAGA Economic Circle, which is a Southeast Asian sub-regional initiative of economic cooperation. It is known as the **Crown Jewel of Mindanao**, being Mindanao island's most important financial and trade center and economically richest city.

Davao is home to the **tallest peak** in the country, **Mt. Apo**. Mountaineers will definitely enjoy the trek to the summit of this **most popular** climbing destination in the country.

Davao is also home to the **Philippine Eagle Center**, where the **largest eagle** in the world, the Philippine eagle, or monkey-eating eagle, is bred in captivity. The Philippine eagle is the country's national bird.

Known as the **Fruit Basket of the Philippines**, its fertile soil produces the **juiciest tropical fruits**, and offers the **cheapest prices** for fresh pomelos, bananas, mangosteen, papayas, mangoes, and probably the **smelliest fruit** in the world, the durian.

Other superlative places to visit include: **Eden Nature Park**, one of the **greenest** ecological tourist spots in the Philippines; **Lon Wa Buddhist Temple**, the **biggest Buddhist temple** in Mindanao; **DECA Wakeboard Park**, the **biggest park** of its kind in the Philippines; and **Gumamela Caverock Farm Resort** which has the **largest Gumamela flower statue**.

Don't leave Davao without, visiting an **orchid farm**, having the freshest, most appetizing grilled **tuna** in the country, and trying the nice beach resorts found on **Samal Island**, just a few minutes boat ride from the mainland.

78.   *Northern Mindanao.* Go on an exotic adventure in Northern Mindanao.

One of the best ways to learn about the tribes of Northern Mindanao is to visit the **Gardens of Malasag Eco-Tourism Village** in **Cagayan de Oro City**. The park features tribal houses and a museum to showcase the rich ethnic heritage of the region. It also showcases the lush ecology of Northern Mindanao through colorful flora and fauna and eco-trails leading to a reforested area. The park also offers a breathtaking view of the **City of Golden Friendship** and **Macajalar Bay**.

Cagayan de Oro is also famous for whitewater rafting at the **Cagayan de Oro River**. The genial, expert river guides make challenging the rapids a most enjoyable thrilling experience for both young and old. Beginner and advanced routes may be booked.

After getting yourself wet during the rafting, hang dry as you go on a zip line and walk over a forest canopy at the **Macahambus Adventure Park**. Purchase a souvenir or two made by the local community to help sustain this noteworthy tourism project.

If you are feeling extra adventurous, visit the **Mapawa Nature Park**, just 11 kilometers from the Cagayan de Oro city proper. The park is a working ranch and reforestation project, and offers thrilling activities like river trekking, swimming in natural spring-fed swimming holes, rappelling alongside a 65-foot waterfall, zip lining, and horseback riding amidst centuries old trees and about 122 indigenous species of flora.

A trip to the cool, rugged mountainous province of **Bukidnon** should also turn out to be a fascinating adventure. It is home to marvelous natural wonders including mountains, canyons, plateaus, waterfalls, and springs. Maybe the best way to experience the beauty of its highlands is to visit the **Dahilayan Adventure Park** in Manolo Fortich. The park boasts of a thrilling 60 to 100 kilometers per hour ride on **Asia's longest Dual Cable Zip line,** 840 meters long dual carrying cables at an elevation drop of 100 meters. A ropes course, zorbing, and a visit to the Forest Park are other activities offered to the bold and daring.

Bukidnon hosts seven indigenous tribes, the **Manobo**, the **Matigsalub**, the **Talaandig**, the **Higaonon**, the **Tigwahanon**, the **Umayamnon,** and the **Bukidnon**, who are headed by *Datus* (Chieftains) and still practice their ancient rituals. Bukidnon celebrates the colorful ethnic customs and traditions of these tribal groups through the **Kaamulan Festival** held from the second half of February and culminating on March 10, the foundation anniversary of the province.

You will be impressed with the **traditional arts and crafts** of the tribal people, through their intricate woven cloth, colorful patchwork and embroidery, and elaborate beadwork.

While in Bukidnon, don't fail to stop at the **Del Monte Pineapple Plantation** in Manolo Fortich. It is one of the biggest pineapple plantations in the world and has a golf course and a clubhouse famous for its tender, lip-smacking steaks. You should also have your fill of the fresh pineapples, the sweetest and juiciest you may ever have in this lifetime.

You can also visit the **Monastery of Transfiguration** in **Malaybalay** for some peace, a glimpse of the monastic life, and a taste of their famous **Monk's Blend** coffee.

Caving and rock climbing are other adventures you can venture in at Bukidnon.

Continue your adventure in the island province of **Camiguin**, located a little to the northeast of Cagayan de Oro. It is a wonder that seven volcanoes, including the still active **Mount Hibok-Hibok**, are found in this smallest province of Northern Mindanao.

Places you should not miss in Camiguin include: **Catarman Church Ruins** and the **Sunken Cemetery**, the remains of a Spanish settlement that lay witness to the devastation brought about by a volcanic eruption in 1871;

the **PHILVOLCS Observatory Station,** which houses a seismograph that monitors of the activity of Mount Hibok-Hibok and from where you can get a stunning view of the island and its surroundings; the **Katibawasan Falls**, a majestic 250-feet waterfall with a rock pool at the base where one can take a dip; and **White Island**, a beautiful white sand bar off the coast of **Mambajao**, the capital of Camiguin.

You can also have your choice between the hot springs of **Ardent** and the cold springs of **Sto. Niño**, or you can do both! Whatever you decide on, you will definitely feel invigorated and refreshed after a dip in the natural spring pools.

79. *Bicol Region.* Spice up your vacation with a visit to this Southeastern Luzon province.

The Bicol Region is best known for the nearly perfect cone of the *Mayon Volcano*, which is accessible via plane or train from Manila to Legazpi City. The volcano is majestic and makes such a beautiful picture. It is, however, the most active volcano in the country and the **Cagsawa Ruins** at its base stands in memory of its wrath.

Mayon Volcano

Mountain climbers will find Mayon truly exciting yet most difficult, with its steep, perilous slopes. It is advised that climbers make arrangements with the Department of Tourism (tourism@albay.gov.ph) before attempting to scale its terrain.

If you are not up to the challenge of strenuous trekking activities, yet would like to experience Mayon up close, there is **Lignon Hill**, which offers the ***Kapit Tuko* (Lizard Grip) Trail that gives a taste** of what it feels like to climb to the summit of Mayon Volcano in 5 to 10 minutes. Visitors may also rent a **4-wheel All-Terrain Vehicle (ATV)** for an adventure ride on the slopes of the volcano to its lava front. An alternative is mountain biking on dried-up gullies at the foothills.

Other exciting activities include a 320-meter zip line, rappelling, and paintball. The less adventurous can take in the superb 360 degree views from the view deck while having some refreshments from the restaurants and shops at the landscaped promenade.

Tourism development has certainly caught up with the province and it has, in the past years, emerged as one of the top tourist destinations in the country.

South of Legazpi City, tourists flock to **Donsol, Sorsogon**, to interact with the **butandings** (whaleshark), called gentle giants as they are, after all, the biggest fish in the world. No, they are not whales, but fish that belong to a variety of sharks that are non-predatory and feed on plankton and small fish. The best time to see them is between February and May. The local community has been organized to operate the boat tours to provide a supplementary income to the fishermen, with the objective of eliminating poaching and hunting of the protected species. Thus, aside from having an amazing experience seeing and swimming with the butandings, you are also helping with the community's conservation efforts.

Diving with manta rays, kayaking, and firefly watching are some of the other activities that can be done around Donsol.

North of Legazpi City is the province of **Camarines Sur**, which has become popular to the international wakeboarding community for the **CamSur Watersports Complex**. It features a 6-point cable ski system and said to be "The Best Cable Park in the World."

Within the area is the **Lago del Rey,** which offers water sports facilities for families - including giant water slides, aqua wall climbing, water polo, water volleyball, kayaking, paddle surfing, boat-towed wakeboarding and skiing, dragon boating, and many others.

East of the province is the **Caramoan**, the *Philippine's Secret Paradise.* It is rightly labeled, as its profound beauty will never fail to inspire awe in any visitor. Island hopping will never be as incredible as when done in Caramoan, with its many idyllic islands offering fine, white sand beaches, mysterious lagoons, grandiose limestone cliffs... all remarkable wonders of nature.

Camarines Sur may be reached by land from Legazpi City or by plane from Manila to **Naga City**.

Catholics or those simply interested in observing religious festivities may find fascinating the **Peñafrancia Festival**, celebrated in honor of the Virgin Mary in Naga City every September. Devotees from all over join in the celebration, which features a fluvial parade (a parade on water, with the revered image, in this case the Virgin Mary, taken aboard a boat, participants also being on boats) and colorful processions. Year-round, pilgrims pay homage to the Our Lady of Peñafrancia at her shrine, as she is believed to have miraculous powers.

When visiting Bicol, be prepared to eat spicy food. Their exotic cuisine includes the pinangat and Bicol Express, which both contain a generous portion of super hot native chili. They even have pizzas with the Bicol Express as topping! Be sure to request mild spice if you are not sure you can take the fiery cuisine. And, remember, the Bicolanos love chili, so there is a big likelihood that mild to them may be too much for you already!

Bicol is also known as the biggest producer of abaca fiber, so be sure to take home fine handicrafts made from the fiber as souvenirs.

TOP SPORTS ACTIVITIES

Because of its natural terrain and resources, the Philippines is a favorite destination for sports enthusiasts, including divers, surfers, golfers, and recently, bikers. Below are the top destinations for said sports activities.

80.   ***Diving.*** Philippine dive sites rival some of the best in the world. The best facet is that you can do diving all year-round! Some of the more popular destinations include:

PALAWAN

Foremost of the many fascinating dive sites is the **Tubbataha Reef** in the Sulu Sea. It can only be reached by live aboard trips, usually from Puerto Princesa City, scheduled between March and June. The terrain is described as varied. The main attraction would be the abundant marine life with giant sharks, groupers, tunas, and mantas.

Northern Palawan also offers fantastic wreck diving in **Coron**, reef diving in **El Nido,** and recreational diving in **Taytay**. Chartered flights are available from Manila.

CENTRAL VISAYAS

Apo Island in **Negros Oriental** offers one of the best diving sites in the Philippines. It is a marine sanctuary and offers vast coral gardens, big drop-offs, impressive walls, and astonishing marine life, including hammerheads, mantas, big-eyed jacks, tuna, and humphead wrasses. It can be reached by boat from Dumaguete City, which is accessible by plane from Manila or fast ferry from Cebu.

Bohol is a favorite destination for divers, with many dive companies servicing the area. The best dive site is around **Balicasag Island**, with the marine sanctuary having beautiful coral gardens. Sightings of schools of hammerheads, big barracudas, game fish and colonies of garden eels are common. Other dive sites are **Cabilao Island** and **Panglao Island**. Bohol is accessible via plane from Manila or fast ferry from Cebu.

In **Cebu**, **Malapascua Island** in the north is popular for its schools of resident thresher sharks.

Down south is **Panagsama Beach** in **Moalboal**, where you can find several dive resorts. From the beach, you can dive at

Pescador Island, where spottings of hammerhead sharks, lionfish, scorpionfish, jacks, pelagic fish, schools of sweetlips, and whale sharks can be expected. Other dive sites from Panagsama Beach are: **Bas Diot**, known for its corals, varied large fish, sea snakes, and underwater caves; **Sa-avedra**, also known for its corals and varied large fish, plus giant sea fans and gorgonians; **Tapanan**, recommended for its coral arches and undersea cliffs; and **Tongo Point** which is easiest to dive during the northeast monsoon (from November to April).

Beginners will enjoy the dive sites off **Mactan Island**, just a few minutes from the airport. Many resorts along the coastline offer diving facilities and lessons. From Mactan, one can go to **Olango Island** and **Pandan Island**, which both offer good recreation dive sites.

Divers may fly direct to Cebu or go via Manila.

SOUTHERN LUZON

Batangas, just 2 to 3 hours by land from Manila, depending on which town you are going to. The towns of **Anilao** and **Nasugbu** both have many good recreational and wreck dive sites.

A ferry ride from Batangas City is **Puerto Galera** in **Oriental Mindoro**. Many foreign divers have set up resorts and dive companies on the island. The recommended dive sites are Escarceo Point, the Canyons, and Shark Cave. The latter is a series of caves where whitetip sharks breed and sleep.

81. **Surfing.** The Philippines offers some nice surf breaks. Although it is not as popular yet as a surfing destination like Hawaii or Indonesia, it has attracted surfers from all over the world, especially those who want to avoid the crowds in the more familiar places. There are surf camps for beginners and international surfing competitions are held at these well-known surfing destinations.

AYE NAVARRO PHOTOGRAPHY

On the northeastern coast of Luzon is **Baler** town in the province of **Aurora**. The trip from Manila may take about 6 hours. Cemento is the most popular break for experienced surfers.

On the northwestern coast of Luzon is **San Fernando** in **La Union**. It is about 5 hour land trip from Manila. Well-known is the Monaliza break.

On the southeastern coast of Luzon is **Catanduanes Island** in **Bicol**. It may be reached by land or plane from Manila. The place is known for its break called Majestic.

On the eastern coast of Mindanao is **Siargao Island** in the province of **Surigao**. It may be reached by plane from Cebu. It may also be reached by plane to Surigao from Manila, then ferry from Surigao to the island. There are many surf spots in this island, the most popular of which is Cloud Nine.

82. ***Golf.*** The Philippines is a golfer's haven. Golf courses designed by famous golf champions abound. The challenges are as diverse as the number of courses, many of which are considered the finest in Asia.

Most of the golf courses are membership clubs but are open to tourists. Most clubs require pre-booking or playing with a member or an endorsement from a member. Inquire from your travel agent and make pre-arrangements. It is also advisable to plan to play on weekdays as weekends, aside from higher green fees, can be crowded and members are given priority.

Conveniently within the city of Manila is the **Club Intramuros**, which, although a short course, presents many challenges, with water hazards and out of bounds. It is open even at night.

Other fine courses in the Metropolis are the **Villamor Golf Course** in Pasay City, a flat course with water hazards and trees, and the 18-hole East and West championship courses of the **Wack Wack Golf and Country Club** in Mandaluyong City.

The provinces of Cavite, Laguna and Batangas, just one and a half to two hours from Manila, offer excellent courses. Foremost of these is the prime **Canlubang Golf and Country Club**, designed by Robert Trent Jones. Indeed of championship tournament design, this is the Philippines' largest and Asia's most challenging. Another worth mentioning is the **Caliraya Springs Golf and Country Club** which is located on the

Caliraya Lake side, designed by Arnold Palmer.

North of Luzon is one of the best in the country, the **Camp John Hay Golf Club** in Baguio, designed by Jack Nicklaus' Golden Bear International. The picturesque rolling hills with lofty pine trees and the cool weather make for an exhilarating game.

Another mountainous course with spectacular views is the **Alta Vista Golf and Country Club** in Cebu. It was designed by Gary Player and The Black Knight. The other course within the city proper is the **Cebu Country Club**, also designed by Gary Player. There are other fine courses in the suburbs, which makes Cebu an ideal golf holiday destination.

In Southern Mindanao, the premier city of Davao also has two beautiful courses that can make the trip well worth it. **Rancho Palos Verdes Golf and Country Club**, designed by Andy Dye, offers varied challenges and provides excellent views of the city. The other is Apo **Golf and Country Club**, named after Mount Apo, a great view of which can be seen from the 10th hole. You can play at the course all year round.

If you are up to combining the pleasures of a beach holiday with golf, then check out the **Fairways and Bluewater Golf and Country**

Club in Boracay Island, designed by Graham Marsh.

83. ***Mountain Climbing, Trekking, and Caving.*** Get rough and take in the scenic topography of the country's highlands.

There are mountains, forests, and caves to explore everywhere. Challenge yourself with a climb up: the tallest Mt. Apo in Davao; the near-perfect cone shaped Mayon Volcano in Bicol; the crater of the smallest Taal Volcano in Batangas; the mighty Mt. Pinatubo in Central Luzon; the sacred Mt. Banahaw in Quezon; the mystical Mt. Pulag in Benguet; and several other enchanting mountains.

Penetrate the caves of Sagada, Siquijor, Cagayan de Oro, Bukidnon, Samar, and many more. Pre-registration with the local government and engagement of local guides are normally required.

The possibilities are endless!

84. ***Biking.*** Owing to the broad range of terrain, the Philippines has varied world-class trails that will surely excite the adventurous mountain biker.

The craze has caught up with Filipinos, and biking groups can be seen traveling to the suburbs on weekends. It is not uncommon to see a car with a mountain bike on top heading out of the city on a Saturday morning or on holidays. Manila urbanites ride their bikes to Tagaytay or to the lakeside towns around the Laguna de Bay.

Sagada Loopers

Extreme riders will be thrilled with the challenge of the slopes of Mayon Volcano in Legazpi City, Mount Pinatubo in Central Luzon, or Mount Apo in Davao.

Cross-country safaris are held in Mindanao, covering Cagayan de Oro, Bukidnon, and Davao.

Other terrific cycling destinations are Cebu, Bohol, Leyte, Samar, and Palawan.

Organized tours from 2 to 15 days are offered by some companies set up by avid bikers. Home-stay or camp facilities are pre-arranged for these tours, complete with an escort vehicle and mechanic in tow.

Most bikers would exclaim that aside from the challenging trails and fantastic views, they are fascinated with the friendliness of the locals.

85. *Running.* Just like biking, running has become increasingly popular among health-conscious Filipinos. It has also become one of the most successful fundraising activities in the country and is highly considered as an effective promotional activity by many companies. There is a running event almost every weekend.

The Philippines has so much more to offer than its diverse natural and man-made tourist attractions. You may want to check out these out of the ordinary activities during this visit.

86. ***Try the Viaje del Sol and Kulinarya Tagala.*** Have a culinary and heritage tour on a day trip from Manila.

    The locales surrounding Laguna de Bay in the National Capital Region have become popular for their magnificent visual and culinary arts. The "Viaje del Sol" (Way of the Sun) features artists' workshops, distinctive restaurants with unique and charming character, and idyllic retreats. Have a feast of the senses with a fill of Filipino artistry and cuisine.

    Start with **Antipolo** and get a breathtaking view of the metropolis. If you are into wooden furniture, make arrangements to visit the beautiful house of sculptor **Benji Reyes**, who is famous for his sculpted wooden furniture made from recycled wood. His pieces are considered investments by collectors from all over.

    Paete is also a must-visit. It has a street lined with shops selling wooden home decors and furnishings and lovely paper mache pieces. You might even find a valuable antique or two.

The **Casa San Pablo** is an inn with sprawling gardens and interesting furnishings and décor, mostly pieces handed down through generations of the owner's family. The ambience is friendly and if you are visiting only for a day, they can provide a home-cooked meal with prior notice.

A visit to the **Collette's Buko Pie Factory** is a true delight. You can see how they make this pastry that is native to Laguna, and get to taste it straight from the oven! Yummy!

Another must stop is the **Kusina Salud**, the country home of famous fashion designer **Patis Tesoro**. Any foodie will enjoy the sumptuous native buffet while dining in a laidback ambience with ornamental and arty curios.

Kinabuhayan Café is another restaurant that offers a unique experience. It is set in a forested area, from where you can trek to waterfalls and caves. The food, prepared by the co-owner and caretaker, **Jay Herrera**, is superb as well!

The **Pettyjohn Pottery Studio** in Bucal, Laguna is the workshop of husband and wife team **Jon and Tessy Pettyjohn**. Make prior reservation so that you can get the chance to see them at work and learn about the potter's process.

Carlito's Workshop in San Pablo, Laguna, on the other hand, is the home of renowned sculptor **Carlito Ortega,** who specializes in welded steel and brass pieces.

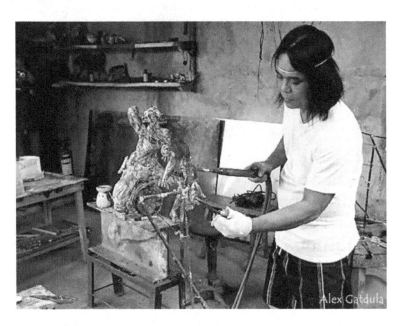
Alex Gatdula

The **Kulinarya Tagala** (Tagalog Culinary) is an organized overnight tour that traverses Laguna, Quezon, and Batangas. The itinerary can be personalized. The regular itinerary includes: breakfast in a 102-yr. old Bahay na Bato (house of stone) and a tour of the Sulyap Gallery Café in San Pablo, Laguna; a pottery demo with buffet lunch at Ugu's Pottery

Garden, considered the best dining experience in this culinary tour; a walking tour along Sariaya, Quezon's heritage area featuring art deco homes; a Tagayan ritual which is a uniquely Quezon wine ritual using the Lambanog (coconut wine) at the Gala-Rodriguez ancestral house; a visit to the Casa Segunda Katigbak ancestral house of the first love of the Philippine national hero, Jose Rizal; a food demonstration by celebrated Chef Pol Poblador; and an overnight stay at a beach resort. Check with your travel agent to book this tour.

87. ***Take a unique Carlos Celdran Tour.*** Celdran calls it "theater at street level".

Carlos Celdran is a performance artist and cultural activist who has been doing walking tours in Intramuros and other parts of downtown Manila in an exceptionally entertaining yet informative way that is uniquely him. He dresses up as a Spanish gentleman for his *Intramuros: If these Walls Could Talk* tour and tells the history of Manila in a dramatic way. The experience is likened to watching a play on foot, with the audience following the actor.

Aside from his Intramuros tour, Celdran has itineraries for Chinatown, Quiapo and Binondo (downtown), Cultural Center Complex, and a tour highlighting the period of the reign of the Marcoses which he calls *Livin La Vida Imelda!,* named after the legendary former First Lady of the Philippines.

Check Celdran's blog for his tour schedules.

88. ***Take a pilgrimage tour.*** Visit centuries old churches and learn about their history and the exquisite architecture as you get closer to the Lord.

Every town and city has its own church, most of which date back to the colonial era. The more common routes are **Southern Cebu** and the **Laguna Loop** (around Laguna de Bay). For small groups, a special tour can be arranged by your tour operator.

89. ***Have your medical needs serviced.*** The Philippines boasts of highly-skilled doctors

and has been a destination for people needing medical treatments. The service is high quality at a much lower cost than in other countries. You can have aesthetic surgeries, dental treatment, eye examinations and treatment, general evaluations, and any other medical needs done while in the country. The government supports medical tourism and many of the bigger hospitals offer packages for tourists.

90.   *Go natural.* Natural health and wellness has undeniably become a new lifestyle trend - and the Philippines is an absolute sanctuary for health and wellness programs.

There are detoxification, weight management, and general wellness programs offered by spa resorts all over the country.

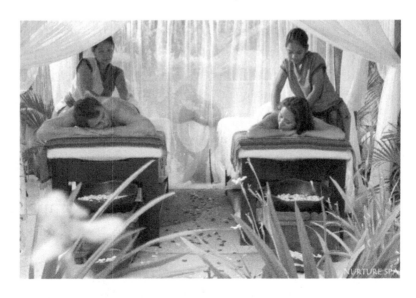

Many tourists, especially from Eastern Europe, and overseas-based Filipinos from Guam and US mainland, come to the Philippines to seek natural healing methods. Because of its biodiversity, natural and herbal medicine is widely available and is a continually growing industry. There are naturopathic doctors, some educated in the U.S., who hold regular clinic and provide personalized programs for ailing patients. Practitioners of alternative healing modalities like acupuncture and the traditional Philippine hilot, traditional therapeutic massage, also offer personalized programs.

There are spa resorts, usually in partnership with natural healing practitioners, who offer in-house programs for those seeking alternative healing methods.

91. *Go to a weekend market.* The weekend markets around Metro Manila present the freshest organic farm produce, seafood, and homemade treats.

For the most part, the vendors are individuals, many of whom are gourmets in their own right, who want to share their love for good eats. There are also small companies working to grow.

The growing crowd of organic food aficionados comes to the weekend markets for their weekly supplies and to get their preserved or pre-cooked favorites.

The most popular are the ones in Makati. The **Salcedo Market**, held every Saturday from 7:00 a.m. to 2:00 p.m. between L.P. Leviste and Tordesillas Streets in Salcedo Village, is a farmers' market with an outdoor deli. **The Legazpi Market**, on the other hand, is open on Sundays from 7:30 a.m. to 2:00 p.m. at the corners of Rufino and Legazpi Streets in Legazpi Village. The latter has handicraft stalls as well as the food.

If you are based at a Makati hotel, you can take a taxi or, if up for a little morning exercise, can get to these markets on foot. You can sample the best family recipes, some passed down for generations. There are also novel foodstuffs, from casseroles to preserved food and baked goodies. It is not farfetched that after sampling an assortment of offerings, you may end up not buying anything, yet be so full you literally have had a free lunch, complete with appetizer, main course, and dessert! Yet, you will for sure not be able to resist buying something to bring back with you! This is truly a pleasurable experience for the foodie.

Another recommended visit for food connoisseurs is the **Mercato Centrale**, held every Saturdays and Sundays from 7:00 a.m. to 2:00 p.m. at the corner of 34th and 8th Street in trendy Bonifacio Global City in Taguig. It was inspired by the outdoor markets of Mercato Centrale in Florence and the Boroughs Market in London, adapted to the local climate by using an air-conditioned tent as a venue. It offers a vibrant food adventure with a wide selection of exciting food finds, a comfortable setting and live entertainment. It even has free Wi-Fi! The busy mom can do her weekend shopping here and bring the whole family for a wonderful experience everyone will enjoy.

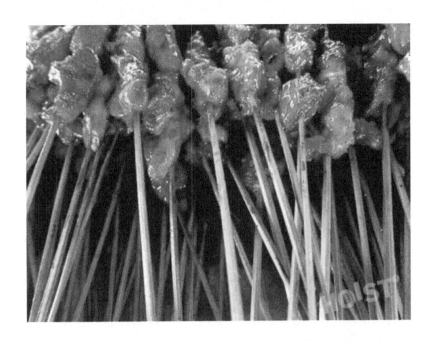

Banchetto, derived from the Italian word which means feast, is exactly that, a feast for the taste buds! The main target market of this market is the call center employees, which is why their operating hours are from 5:00 p.m. to 7:00 a.m. on Fridays. The venue is the tent at the corner of Meralco Avenue in Ortigas Center, Pasig. Banchetto offers a vibrant dining experience for night owls.

Because of the favorable turn-out of patrons not only from the call center industry but also from the neighboring communities, Banchetto has expanded to operate Overnight Roadside Food Fiestas in two other locations. **Banchetto FORUM** is now open every Wednesday and Thursday night from 8:30 p.m. until 6:00 a.m. at the delivery bay area of Robinson's Pioneer corner EDSA in

Mandaluyong City, while **Banchetto LIBIS** is open every Tuesday night from 6:00 p.m. until 4:00 a.m. at the open parking area of Shopwise in Libis, Quezon City.

South of Manila is **Soderno, held on Saturdays and Sundays from 7:00 a.m. to 4:00 p.m. at the** Molito Lifestyle Center at the corner of Madrigal and Commerce Avenue in the upscale area of Alabang, Muntinlupa. Handicrafts, dry goods, and to-go food are featured on Saturdays, while organic produce are featured on Sundays. As in the other markets, the sellers are entrepreneurs introducing their unique products.

92. ***Take a crack at Karaoke.*** Never mind if you can't carry a tune, you will still have a blast singing along with the Filipinos!

Filipinos are known for their musicality and LOVE to sing. It is not surprising that a Filipino invented the sing-along system called Minus One which is now commonly called the karaoke machine.

Karaoke is a favorite pastime of Filipinos, and almost all parties incorporate karaoke singing in the program. You can find a karaoke bar even in the most remote areas. There are high end bars that offer private rooms that can be rented on an hourly basis. You can then belt out to your heart's desire without having to wrestle for the microphone. Sing as if you have no care in the world and feel any stress desert your body.

Check first with your hotel concierge for information on a decent, wholesome place to go.

93. ***Go footloose with the Cebu Dancing Inmates.*** Have the rare opportunity to dance with Cebu's famous Dancing Inmates.

The Cebu Dancing Inmates became a viral sensation in 2007 when a video of their performance, all 1500 of them, dancing to Michael Jackson's *Thriller*, was uploaded on You Tube. It has a staggering over 50 million views already. Watch the original upload at http://www.youtube.com/watch?v=hMnk7lh 9M3o

In 2010, Jackson's choreographer, Travis Pane, trained the inmates the dance routines of *The Drill* to the tune of *They Don't Care About Us. The Drill* is a scene in the *This is it* film tribute to Michael Jackson.

The Cebu Provincial Detention and Rehabilitation Center (CPDRC) has adopted dance as part of its rehabilitation program. It started as an alternative to the regular morning exercises to keep the prisoners physically and mentally fit. Needless to say, it has succeeded not only in engaging the prisoners in a coordinated presentation, but also in making them feel a sense of being appreciated. They are probably one of the best examples of why *It is more fun in the Philippines* and are now one of the most unique top tourist attractions.

The Cebu Dancing Inmates perform every last Saturday of the month for free. After the program, the audience is invited to go down from the stands and join the inmates in some dance moves. Visitors are also encouraged to support the program by buying some souvenirs made by the inmates themselves. Contact the CPDRC at (+6332) 255-3673 for confirmation of show schedule.

94. ***Take a community-based tour or eco-tour.*** You can do your part in helping make tourism sustainable.

There are many community-based tourism initiatives in the country. You might want to try **whale and/or dolphin watching**, which are mostly operated by local governments. The boat crew members are usually former whale hunters trained as spotters in a bid to preserve the environment. The operational whale and/or dolphin watching communities include Donsol, Sorsogon in the Bicol Region, Pamilacan in Bohol, Barangay Tulingan, Puerto Princesa in Palawan, and Oslob in Cebu.

Also in Bohol is the **Oyster Farm Tour** organized by the riverbank Cambuhat Village. This tour involves everyone in the community. The men bring you on a paddleboat ride to the oyster farm and give you a background on oyster culture, while the women prepare the seafood lunch, of course with oysters in the menu. Local talents entertain you with native songs and poetry while you dine al fresco. You will also get to tour the village and see villagers during their loom weaving and broom making activities.

River cruises are offered by organized local communities in Tagum, Davao Del Norte, just an hour drive from Davao City, and in Boho, Aloguinsan, Cebu.

Firefly watching is offered by the Iwahig community in Puerto Princesa, Palawan, and by the local government in Sorsogon, while **bird watching** is offered by the Olango Island fishing community in Cebu.

Mangrove tours are offered in Panadtaran by the Candijay town, Bohol and at the Talabong Mangrove Park in Bais, Negros Oriental. Both are educational eco-tours that are sure to delight.

A **tribal exposure tour** is offered at the Bagobo Tribal Village in Tibolo, Santa Cruz, Davao del Sur. The villagers show you

119

traditional abaca weaving and beadwork and serve you a local meal. You also get to meet Datu Ruben who heads the tribe.

If you just want a short introduction within the confines of Davao City, there is a Bagobo sub-tribe composed of descendants of Datu Udang, who welcome visitors to their home. They provide a background on the customs and traditions of the tribe and serve a traditional snack spread. The Datu's grandchildren don tribal attire and perform dances depicting the time-honored rituals of the tribe. Although the tribe now lives in a modern environment, Mrs. Udang is determined to preserve the traditions through the community's younger generation.

Farm tours allow you to enjoy the vast agricultural landscape while learning how the food you eat is produced. Such tours are operated in many areas of the Philippines including Bulacan, Guimaras, Zambales, and Bukidnon. The one in Danao, Bohol is operated by a farmers' foundation.

There are many other community-based tours and eco-tours in the country. All the tours require pre-arrangement. Contact a Department of Tourism (DOT) accredited tour operator in the locality for assistance.

Visit http://www.visitmyphilippines.com/ for further information on the varied offerings of the different Philippine regions.

RECOMMENDATIONS FROM LOCALS

95. ***Cool off on a hot day with halo-halo.*** Halo is a Tagalog word which means mix, thus halo-halo means a mix. Aptly named, it is a mix of caramelized bananas and sweet potato, preserved beans and coco gel, and other delicacies with shaved ice, milk and sugar, or honey. The "special variety is usually topped off with a scoop or two of ice cream. It is a refreshing dessert that anyone with a sweet tooth will surely love.

96. ***Endeavor to try purple colored desserts.***
Try a variety of purple-colored desserts made
from ube, the local name for purple yam, a
lavender colored rootcrop. You may find the
color strange for ice cream, but the
Philippines' ube ice cream is very popular and
a must try. The ube is also used for jams,
candies, cakes and pastries.

97. ***Taste Pan de Sal dipped in coffee.***
Considered the Filipino roll bread, pan de sal
(bread of salt) is usually served during
breakfast or as an afternoon snack with
butter or cheese. It is available fresh from the
oven in many small bakeries around any
neighborhood, usually early morning and
mid-afternoon. It is best taken hot and goes
well with any spread. Many Filipinos love to
dip their pan de sal in their coffee before
biting into it.

98. ***Try San Miguel Beer Pale Pilsen.*** This pale, golden lager originates in the Philippines. It is one of the finest and one of the largest selling beers worldwide. It is well balanced and subtle with a great taste and aroma. The San Miguel Brewery also offers Premium All-Malt Beer, Super Dry, Cerveza Negra, Light, and Flavored variants. It also produces two strong beer varieties, Red Horse and Gold Eagle.

99. ***Dare to eat balut***. Balut is a local delicacy that is nothing more than duck egg with a fertilized embryo that is boiled. Definitely only for the bold at heart and stomach, it is eaten warm and in the shell. It is sold by vendors around the city streets at night and is a nourishing snack that is high in protein and is popularly believed to be an aphrodisiac. It is highly probable that it is sold in the evenings as it is best eaten in the dark so you do not see what it looks like! You can take it with rock salt or chili vinegar, and is great with beer. However, if you are watching your cholesterol level, then you have an excuse not to try it.

100. *Have a Fun Ride on a Calesa.* The calesa or karitela is a horse-drawn carriage that was the main mode of transport in the 18th century driven by a kutsero. Some still exist in downtown Manila. Calesas are also available for tours around the Walled City of Intramuros. They are also a convenient way to get around the heritage town of Vigan in Ilocos, Sur. Riding in one is a wonderful photo opportunity, as the calesas are usually very colorful.

There you go... 100 tips in traveling to the Philippines.

Whatever you are inclined to travel for, you will find it in one of the 7,107 islands. One may never be able to uncover all the wonders the Philippines has to offer in a lifetime, but the most valuable experience may be your encounters with the Filipinos.

So what are you waiting for? Begin your journey to discover why *It is more fun in the Philippines!*

ACKNOWLEDGEMENT

My loving husband Carlo, children, and siblings have been so supportive of this endeavor, and I wish to thank them for cheering me on in my first attempt at writing a book. I suspect they were as excited as I was. Special thanks to my daughter Nadine, who patiently helped with the layout.

I would also like to mention my friends who have always expressed confidence in my abilities and have influenced me to pursue my passion for writing: Liz Maloles, whom I credit for leading me to this road; E. J. McKnight for the constant encouragement and grammar check; Keiko Quintana for her patience in reading the draft and giving honest criticism; Ricky Tio for all the opportunities he sends my way; and Eddie Nuque for being my forever tourism mentor.

My appreciation also goes to my friends at PDP Digital, Inc., TPC lente photography group, my relatives and other friends, who share the same love for the Philippines as I, and were so generous to furnish or help solicit photographs and ideas for use in the book.

Most of all, I will be forever grateful to Jessie Voigts and Ed Forteau of Wandering Educators, who believed in me and gave me the opportunity to share the beauty of our islands in this book. And of course, to Beth Whitman, who introduced me to Jessie and Ed and to the world of writing.

Rissa Gatdula-Lumontad

Authers

Rissa Gatdula-Lumontad is a Filipino mother, wife and tourism professional based in Manila, Philippines. She has a career in the Philippine tourism industry that spans more than 15 years. She has been to many parts of the Philippine islands in her quest to develop new products to offer tourists as part of her job. Whenever she can, she brings her family along to expose her children to the world outside of home and school as she believes that traveling is the best way for them to learn. Further, she finds family travel an excellent and fun bonding opportunity.

At present, Rissa works from home doing tours and events consulting and virtual assistance, including some writing for foreign executives. Writing this book is a fulfillment of her desire to share the Philippines with the rest of the world.

Dr. Jessie Voigts is a mom who loves sharing the world with her daughter. She has a PhD in International Education, and is constantly looking for ways to increase intercultural understanding, especially with kids (it's never too young to start!). She has lived and worked in Japan and London, and traveled around the world. Jessie and her family live on a lake in Michigan, enjoying the summers swimming, kayaking, and sailing, and planning travel for the winter months. Jessie is the publisher of WanderingEducators.com, a travel site for global educators, and with Wandering Educators Press, has published six books on travel and intercultural learning, with more on the way.

Photo Credits:

Cover - Fun on Calesa, Manila: TPC lente-Pepper Manuel

Mabuhay!, SM Mall of Asia, Pasay City: TPC lente-Carlo Lumontad

Family Carousel Fun, Enchanted Kingdom: Kyle Lumontad

Snorkeling, Boracay: NeNaNi Events

Masskara Festival, Bacolod City: PDP Digital, Inc.-Daniel Carpentier

Night Skyline, Manila City: TPC lente-Paulimar Gene Aranco

Airplane for Domestic Flight, NAIA 3: TPC lente-Eric Tanyen

U.S. Dollars, Cash: NeNaNi Events-Rissa Lumontad

Skyline, Makati City: Dos Litratistas/TPC lente-Royce Malacaman

Cool Mountains, Northern Luzon: NeNaNi Events

Interior of Basilica Minore del Sto. Niño, Cebu City: TPC lente-Pepper Manuel

Girl at Kalilangan Festival, General Santos City: TPC lente-Eric Tanyen

Lady in Filipiniana Dress, Philippine Modernized Costume: TPC lente-Alvin Rivero

Man in Barong Tagalog, Philippine Formal Attire: TPC lente-Annie Fajardo

Jeepney, Philippine Mode of Transport: Dos Litratistas/TPC lente-Royce Malacaman

Bus Station, Quezon City: TPC lente-Danedherson Garcia

LRT, Manila: TPC lente-John Rudio

PNR Trains, Manila: TPC lente-Vipee Flores

Inter-island Plane, Manila Domestic Airport:
   Nathan Javier
Bangkas (Pumpboats), Mactan Island, Cebu:
   NeNaNi Events-Rissa Lumontad
Beach Resort, Mactan Island, Cebu: NeNaNi
   Events-Rissa Lumontad
Beach Resort, Boracay Island: TPC lente-Eric
   Suarez
*Tapsilog (Cured Beef, Fried Rice and Egg),
   Philippine Rice Meal*: TPC lente-Jec Santiago
Delectable Kare-Kare, Filipino Food: TPC lente-
   Jec Santiago
Mouthwatering Lechon, Filipino Food: TPC lente-
   Dhen Pajarillo
Fresh Seafood, Dining in the Philippines: Nathan
   Javier
Peaceful Beach Scene, General Santos City: TPC
   lente-Eric Tanyen
Rafting with Small Child, Cagayan de Oro: Cebu
   Holiday Tours/NeNaNi Events
Horseback Riding, Baguio: TPC lente-Carlo
   Lumontad
SM Mall of Asia, Pasay City: TPC lente-Pepper
   Manuel
Tyangge, Cebu: TPC lente-Carlo Lumontad
Fort Santiago, Intramuros, Manila: Dos
   Litratistas/TPC lente-Royce Malacaman
Rizal Monument, Manila: NeNaNi Events
Manila Bay Sunset, Pasay City: TPC lente-Chris
   Vergara
Taal Volcano and Lake, Taal, Batangas: Nathan
   Javier
Banaue Rice Terraces, Ifugao Province: Nathan
   Javier

Igorot Native Costume, Baguio: TPC lente-Carlo Lumontad

Underground River, Puerto Princesa, Palawan: Christopher E. Cruz

Snake Island, Honda Bay, Puerto Princesa, Palawan: Christopher E. Cruz

Beachfront, Boracay Island: NeNaNi Events-Rissa Lumontad

Barefoot Walk Along the White Sand Beachfront, Boracay Island: TPC lente-Chi Payba

Seawalk, Boracay: NeNaNi Events

Magellan's Cross Monument, Cebu City: TPC lente-Carlo Lumontad

Resort Beachfront, Mactan Island, Cebu: NeNaNi Events-Rissa Lumontad

Chocolate Hills, Bohol: Nathan Javier

Tarsier, Bohol: TPC lente-Fernando Caliza

River Cruise Lunch, Loboc River, Bohol: Nathan Javier

Calle Crisologo, Vigan: Jim Bernardo

Bangui Windmills, Ilocos Norte: Jim Bernardo

Philippine Eagle, Davao City: TPC lente-Eric Tanyen

At the Summit of Mt. Apo, Davao City: Jerson Pikes

Kaamulan Festival, Bukidnon: Atoy Martinez

White Water Rafting, Cagayan de Oro: Cebu Holiday Tours/NeNaNi Events

Tribal Warriors, Kaamulan Festival, Bukidnon: Atoy Martinez

Rappelling from Waterfalls, Mapawa Nature and Adventure Park, Cagayan de Oro: Iggy Pelaez

Majestic Mayon Volcano, Albay: PDP Digital, Inc.-Daniel Carpentier

Whaleshark Interaction, Oslob, Cebu: Erwin T. Lim

Knee Boarding, Camsur Watersports Complex, Camarines Sur: Cebu Holiday Tours

Fish and Ocean Flora, Manila Ocean Park, Manila: TPC lente-Pepper Manuel

Dive Resort, Alona Beach, Panglao Island, Bohol: Nathan Javier

Surfing, Siargao Island, Surigao del Norte: Aye Navarro

Tourist Golf Swing, Golfing: Standing Ovations

Mountaineer's View from Atop, Mt. Pulag, Benguet: Jerson Pikes

Mountain Biking, Sagada, Mountain Province: Sagada Loopers

Casa San Pablo, Laguna: NeNaNi Events-Rissa Lumontad

Collette's Buko Pie Factory, San Pablo City, Laguna: Alex Gatdula

Sculptor at Work, Carlito's Workshop, San Pablo City, Laguna: Alex Gatdula

Carlos Celdran in Action, Intramuros, Manila: Ka Bino Guerrero

Wellness Treatment, Nurture Spa Village, Tagaytay: Nurture Spa Village

Caesar's Salad, Weekend Market: TPC lente-Jec Santiago

Pork Barbecue on Sticks, Filipino Food: Nathan Javier

Dancing with Cebu Dancing Inmates, Cebu City: NeNaNi Events

Firefly Watching, Sorsogon: Cebu Holiday Tours-Ricky Tio

Scrumptious Halo-Halo, Local's Recommendations: TPC lente-Annie Fajardo

Pan de Sal and Coffee, Local's Recommendations: TPC lente-Carlo Lumontad

Calesa, Intramuros, Manila: Dos Litratistas/TPC lente-Royce Malacaman